SYDNEY

PHILIP STEELE

WORLD ALMANAC® LIBRARY

Please visit our web site at: www.worldalmanaclibrary.com
For a free color catalog describing World Almanac® Library's list of high-quality books
and multimedia programs, call 1-800-848-2928 (USA) or 1-800-387-3178 (Canada).
World Almanac® Library's fax: (414) 332-3567.

Library of Congress Cataloging-in-Publication Data available upon request from publisher.
Fax (414) 336-0157 for the attention of the Publishing Records Department.

ISBN 0-8368-5032-7 (lib. bdg.)
ISBN 0-8368-5192-7 (softcover)

First published in 2004 by
World Almanac® Library
330 West Olive Street, Suite 100
Milwaukee, WI 53212 USA

Copyright © 2004 by World Almanac® Library.

Produced by Discovery Books
Editor: Helen Dwyer
Series designers: Laurie Shock, Keith Williams
Designer and page production: Keith Williams
Photo researcher: Rachel Tisdale
Maps and diagrams: Stefan Chabluk
World Almanac® Library editorial direction: Mark J. Sachner
World Almanac® Library editor: Jenette Donovan Guntly
World Almanac® Library art direction: Tammy Gruenewald
World Almanac® Library production: Jessica Morris

Photo credits: AKG-Images: p.10; Art Directors & Trip: pp.15, 19, 27, 36, 37; Art Directors & Trip/Eric Smith: Cover, title
page, p.40; Art Directors & Trip/Australian Picture Library: p.4; Chris Fairclough Photography: pp.11, 23, 25, 41; Corbis:
pp.7, 26; Corbis/Eye Ubiquitous/ Matthew McKee: p.32; Corbis/Hulton Deutsch Collection: p.14; Corbis/Paul A. Souders:
p.38; Corbis/Sygma/John Van Hasselt: pp.16, 35; David Simson – DASPHOTOGB@aol.com: p.42; Eye Ubiquitous/
Matthew McKee: pp.30, 43; Eye Ubiquitous/Paul Thompson: p.18; James Davis Travel Photography: pp.22, 34; James Davis
Worldwide: p.24; Mary Evans Picture Library: pp.8, 12; Panos Pictures/Brian Goddard: p.31; Panos Pictures/Liba Taylor: p.20;
Still Pictures/Jochen Tack: p.29

**Cover caption: A view of downtown Sydney shows its harbor from the southeast with the Domain and the Royal Botanic
Gardens in the foreground.**

Printed in the United States of America

1 2 3 4 5 6 7 8 9 08 07 06 05 04

Contents

Introduction

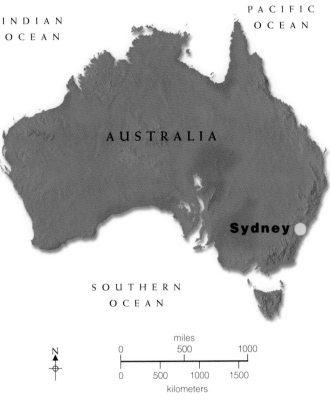

INDIAN OCEAN

PACIFIC OCEAN

AUSTRALIA

Sydney

SOUTHERN OCEAN

miles
0   500   1000

0   500   1000   1500
kilometers

N

Australia is a sparsely populated land of desert, rock, scrub, and forest. Much of it is wilderness, or "bush." There are huge sheep stations and rolling farmland, too, but only along the coastline do you find Australia's big cities.

The biggest of these is Sydney, capital of the state of New South Wales in southeastern Australia. With a population of

◄ *Sydney Harbour Bridge (opened in 1932) accommodates a railroad track, eight lanes of freeway, a cycle lane, and a sidewalk. Its massive steel arch gives it the nickname of the "coat hanger."*

about 4 million, Sydney is a little larger than Melbourne, located in the neighboring state of Victoria to the south. There is an old rivalry between the two cities, yet neither is the national capital. That honor belongs to a much smaller city to the south of Sydney, Canberra, which was established in 1927.

However, Sydney is a splendid, world-class city, built around a natural harbor. While northern parts of the world are experiencing winter snowfall, Sydney is enjoying the southern summer, with January temperatures averaging 71° Fahrenheit (22° Celsius). Intense heat causes bushfires in the surrounding countryside, and these sometimes threaten life and property on the edges of Sydney's suburbs. The southern winters are cooler, with a 53° F (12° C) average in July. When it does rain, it pours, bringing the average yearly precipitation up to 47 inches (120 centimeters).

A City by the Sea

The harbor, with its coves, headlands, and small islands, is dotted with yachts and pleasure boats and crossed by ferries and cruise liners. The Sydney Opera House clings to the harbor's southern shore, which is the heart of Sydney. The city extends northward, too, linked to the southern shore by the Sydney Harbour Tunnel and Bridge.

The oldest district, known as the Rocks, huddles under the southern end of the Sydney Harbour Bridge. Today, cruise liners anchor offshore, and local ferryboats dock along the piers of Circular Quay, a place

CITY FACTS

Sydney
Capital of the State
of New South Wales, Australia

Founded: A.D. 1788

Area: 1,411 square miles
(3,655 square kilometers)

Population: 3,997,321
(2001 census)

Population Density:
2,833 people per square mile
(1,094 per sq km)

"In Sydney Harbour...the yachts will be racing on the crushed diamond water under a sky the texture of powdered sapphires."

—Clive James, Australian writer, 1980.

always crowded with businesspeople, tourists, traders, and entertainers, including very often an Aborigine playing a didgeridoo. The booming, rhythmic tones of this large, wooden trumpet belong to another, more ancient Australia.

Modernity takes hold once more among the high-rise buildings, offices, hotels, and shops of the Central Business District, which stretches along George Street and Pitt Street. Darling Harbour forms the western edge of this district.

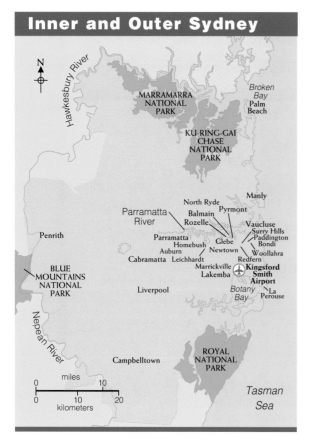

Inner and Outer Sydney

N

Hawkesbury River

MARRAMARRA NATIONAL PARK

Broken Bay
Palm Beach

KU-RING-GAI CHASE NATIONAL PARK

Manly

North Ryde
Pyrmont
Parramatta River
Balmain
Rozelle
Vaucluse
Surry Hills
Paddington
Bondi
Parramatta
Homebush
Glebe
Newtown
Woollahra
Auburn
Cabramatta
Leichhardt
Redfern
Marrickville
Kingsford
Smith
Airport
Lakemba

Penrith

BLUE MOUNTAINS NATIONAL PARK

Liverpool
Botany Bay
La Perouse

Nepean River

Campbelltown

ROYAL NATIONAL PARK

Tasman Sea

miles
0   10
0   10   20
kilometers

Sydney City Center

N

Sydney Harbour Bridge
Sydney Harbour Tunnel
Port Jackson
Bennelong Point
Sydney Opera House

The Rocks
Sydney Cove

Museum of Contemporary Art
Circular Quay

Farm Cove
The Domain

Conservatorium of Music

Darling Harbour

Australian National Maritime Museum
George St.
Pitt St.
Martin Place
GPO
Sydney Aquarium
Strand Arcade

Castlereagh St.
Elizabeth St.
Macquarie St.

Royal Botanic Gardens
State Library
Parliament House

St. James Church
The Domain
Art Gallery of New South Wales

Pyrmont Bridge

Queen Victoria Building
St. Mary's Cathedral

Town Hall
Hyde Park

Bathurst St.
St Andrew's Cathedral
Australian Museum
Anzac War Memorial

Kings Cross

Darling Harbour
Monorail
Liverpool St.
Oxford St.

Powerhouse Museum
Chinese Gardens

University of Technology
Central Station
Eddy Ave.

Ultimo

Park areas

miles
0   0.5
0   0.5
kilometers

Macquarie Street marks the eastern border of the Central Business District. Bounded to the east by the Royal Botanic Gardens and a large park named the Domain, it includes many of Sydney's oldest and most important public buildings.

The Royal Botanic Gardens, with their palms and gum trees, were laid out by Governor Lachlan Macquarie in 1816. The gardens border Farm Cove, the site of the first fields farmed by British settlers. To the south is the green space of the Domain, which is popular with picnickers. Southeast of the Domain is the long strip of Hyde Park, with its grand fountain and war memorial. To the east of these parks is Woolloomooloo Bay ("the 'Loo"), formerly the chief point of arrival for passenger ships.

Sydney's Suburbs

In its streets and architecture, Sydney is very much the creation of its nineteenth-century British settlers. Hyde Park, Kings Cross, Oxford Street, Liverpool Street, Paddington, and Haymarket are all names in London, England, as well as in Sydney.

The inner suburbs vary greatly, each having its own unique character. There is run-down Kings Cross, fashionable Paddington, the row houses of Surry Hills,

Opera on the Shore

Bennelong Point is named after the Aborigine who first explained the customs of his people to the British settlers. Today, it is the site of one of the world's most instantly recognizable landmarks, the Sydney Opera House (above). The flyaway design of its white roofs has become a symbol of the new Australia. The building was designed by Danish architect Jørn Utzon and was heavily criticized during its construction for being too modern and too expensive. However, the people of Sydney soon realized, after its completion in 1973, that this graceful structure was one of the city's greatest assets.

Newtown with its student housing, leafy Glebe with its cafés, and Balmain, a working-class area now taken over by arts and media people. In the east is the wealthy old suburb of Vaucluse and cheerful Bondi, with its beach, which is famous with surfers worldwide. The North Shore has some of the city's most expensive newer properties with the best harbor views.

The suburbs cover most of the coastal plain east of the Blue Mountains. At their greatest extent eastward, they stretch to the suburb of Penrith and the Nepean River. They also extend northward to Ku-Ring-Gai Chase National Park and Palm Beach and southward beyond Liverpool to Campbelltown.

CHAPTER 1

History of Sydney

The Aborigines were the first Australians, settling the vast landmass at least 50,000 years ago. By the time the British arrived in Australia, there were about 650 widely scattered Aboriginal groups. They lived by fishing, hunting, gathering, and farming. They carved or painted pictures on the rocks, including designs of kangaroos, hunters, and canoes. In the Sydney area, about 2,000 examples of rock art have survived, and in Sydney Harbour National Park alone, about 70 surviving sites are associated with the Aborigines.

British Colonists Arrive

In the 1600s and 1700s, Europeans explored the Australian coast. In 1770, the English sea captain James Cook landed in Botany Bay and claimed the land for Great Britain, naming it New South Wales. The British government decided it would be an ideal place to found a penal colony (a settlement where prisoners were detained and punished). Politicians thought this was a way of reducing crime at home and would also help the economy of British colonies overseas.

◀ English navigator Captain James Cook came ashore at Botany Bay on April 28, 1770. Sticking the British flag in the ground, he claimed the newly discovered land for Great Britain.

> *"We had the satisfaction of finding the finest natural harbor in the world, in which a thousand ships of the line may ride in the most perfect security."*
>
> —Captain Arthur Phillip, 1788.

The first fleet arrived in 1788, commanded by Captain Arthur Phillip. His 11 ships contained 664 marines, sailors, government officials and their families, and 821 convicts. Some of the prisoners had only been found guilty of petty crimes such as small-scale theft. Many Irish people were sent for having a rebellious attitude toward the English. Some English people were transported for political activity. After they had served their sentences, the prisoners would be freed. Botany Bay proved to be far from ideal on closer inspection, so Phillip sailed around into the inlet of Port Jackson, a short distance to the north, and set up a camp of tents in Sydney Cove.

The colonists had brought with them all sorts of plants, seeds, and livestock, but the early years were hard, and many went hungry. Starvation was a constant fear, and food was strictly rationed. A second fleet arrived in 1790 after a grim voyage in which one-fourth of the convicts died. Free settlers only began to arrive after 1793. By then, convicts had labored to put up the first buildings of brick and stone.

Most Aborigines were unsure how to treat the invaders. Some, led by a warrior called Pemulwuy, offered resistance, but, armed only with clubs, wooden swords, and spears, they stood little chance against guns and steel weapons. Many more died of European diseases, such as smallpox, to which they had no immunity.

The Aborigines were not recognized as owners of the land on which they lived. Although the British government gave the settlers instructions to treat the Aborigines well, many of the newcomers were racists, and the original Australians were soon doomed to a wretched existence in their own land. Some Aborigines fled into the country's interior, but as settlers spread out through New South Wales, Aborigines were often gunned down and hunted like animals, or their water supplies were poisoned.

City Names

Many Aboriginal place names still appear on the map of Sydney, such as Woollahra, Parramatta, Woolloomooloo, Narrabeen, and Taronga. Sydney itself was named after a British politician, Viscount Sydney. Some districts and streets are named after other people who made their mark on the city's history, such as Lachlan Macquarie (the British governor from 1810–1821), William Redfern (the founder of healthcare in Australia), and Ludwig Leichhardt (a Prussian explorer and naturalist who led expeditions across Australia in the 1840s).

Early Days

After Captain Phillip left Sydney in December 1792, life in the settlement deteriorated. The convicts were harshly and cruelly treated. They spent their days in hard labor and slept in rat-infested, crowded barracks. Flogging was a common punishment. Government of the colony was weak, allowing army officers and leading settlers to engage in corruption and profiteering.

In 1810, Lachlan Macquarie became governor of the wider region of New South Wales. By the time of his departure in 1821, Macquarie had transformed Sydney and turned around its fortunes. He organized land surveys and the building of roads. Firm but fair, Macquarie ordered that Aborigines should be treated the same as Europeans. While Macquarie was governor, the population of New South Wales tripled. The Australian interior was explored, and new penal colonies were set up in Tasmania and Queensland, while free settlements were established at Perth, Melbourne, and Adelaide. One by one, these broke away to be governed as separate British colonies.

Sydney Expands

The last convicts arrived in Sydney in 1840. From 1832 to 1851, the British government gave financial help to those wishing to

◀ *A late nineteenth-century woodcut depicts an Aboriginal woman cradling her baby. European settlement disrupted a unique way of life that had developed over many thousands of years.*

emigrate freely to Australia, so the British population of Sydney grew and grew. There were 95,000 people in Sydney by 1861 and 399,000 by 1891. The 1 million mark was passed in 1925, and the 2 million mark in 1963.

The new Australian economy depended on wool, and the ideal breed of sheep for the New South Wales grasslands proved to be the Spanish Merino. Coal was another source of wealth. In 1851, gold was discovered in Bathurst, 100 miles

The Oldest Home

Although much of the unhealthy Rocks district was pulled down in 1900, following an outbreak of disease, Cadman's Cottage (above) remains — the oldest surviving home in Sydney. It is a small, two-story stone house located by the former seawall, built in 1815 for government boat crews. From 1827, it was the home of John Cadman, a convict transported for horse theft who became superintendent of government boats for the settlement.

▲ *The famous clipper ship* Cutty Sark *(center) loads up with wool at Sydney's Circular Quay in 1880.*

(161 km) inland from Sydney. Settlers, prospectors, and miners swarmed through the city in search of a fortune.

Sydney remained Australia's chief port. Fast clippers (large, streamlined sailing ships) such as the *Cutty Sark*, built in 1869, could carry cargoes of wool from Sydney to London under full sail in just seventy-three days. The first fleet of ships had taken eight months to complete the journey

"[Sydney in the 1880s and 1890s] was its best, a city that will never again be seen on Earth — a sailor-town city, a free-trade city, a pre-mechanized city, in which jostled in lower George Street and the Quay sailors from all the Earth, and glimpsed over wharves and the roofs of harbor-side houses the tall spars of sailing ships."

—Norman Lindsay, Australian writer and painter, 1957.

in 1787–1788. By the 1880s, advances in refrigeration technology allowed meat to be exported.

The city itself was changing rapidly. Around the wharves, the Rocks became a rough docklands district, but elsewhere, mud-brick structures gave way to grand stone public buildings, arch-covered streets full of shops, parks, and churches. Paddle steamers were crossing the harbor by 1831, and a regular ferry service to the northern suburb of Manly started twenty years later. The railroad reached the outer western suburb of Parramatta in 1855 and, along with streetcars, made commuting possible, leading to the building of new suburbs. Sydney became one of the chief cities of the all-powerful British Empire.

The Early Twentieth Century

By 1901, ships could unload at 23 miles (37 km) of wharves. That was the year in which a united federation of the British colonies — the Commonwealth of Australia — came into being.

Sydney's men left to fight for the British Empire in World War I, and many died in a disastrous assault on the Gallipoli Peninsula in Turkey in 1915–1916. This tragedy was followed by much bitterness and a savage, drunken riot by army recruits broke out on the streets of Sydney.

Sydney suffered greatly during the worldwide economic problems of the 1920s and 1930s. Banks crashed, United States loans to Europe ended, trade with

"[Sydney] is shaped somewhat like an oak-leaf — a roomy sheet of lovely blue water, with narrow off-shoots of water running up into the country on both sides between long fingers of land, high wooded ridges with sides sloped like graves. Handsome villas are perched here and there on these ridges, snuggling amongst the foliage, and one catches alluring glimpses of them as the ship swims by toward the city. The city clothes a cluster of hills and a ruffle of neighboring ridges with its undulating masses of masonry, and out of these masses spring towers and spires and other architectural dignities and grandeurs that break the flowing lines and give picturesqueness to the general effect."

—Mark Twain, in *Following the Equator, A Journey Around the World*, 1897.

Australia shrank, Australian industrial output fell, and unemployment rose. Many citizens were homeless and hungry. Some unemployed workers turned to radical politics. The trade unions, which had been growing in power since the 1890s, now

became a major force in city politics. They remained so for the following fifty years.

As air travel grew in the 1930s, it became easier for people from Great Britain to travel to Australia. Flying boats from Europe could land on Rose Bay, close to the center of the city. In World War II (1939–1945), Australia fought for its survival as Japan invaded neighboring lands in Southeast Asia. Japanese submarines cruised as far south as Sydney, and in 1942, they launched a raid on ships moored in Woolloomooloo, right by the city center.

The Birth of Modern Sydney

From 1947 onward, many Europeans displaced from their homes by the war came to Sydney, looking forward to rebuilding their lives on the other side of the world. They were followed by large numbers of new immigrants from Great Britain.

However, World War II had shifted Sydney's focus away from distant Great Britain to its geographical location on the edge of the Pacific Ocean. The economy of this region, known as the Pacific Rim, took off in the decades after World War II after the departure of European powers from their colonies in Southeast Asia. Huge economic growth took place in Japan and Taiwan in the 1950s and 1960s, in South Korea in the 1960s and 1970s, and later in Hong Kong, Singapore,

◄ *In 1942, civilians were evacuated from their homes when Sydney was shelled by a Japanese submarine.*

◄ *A Pool of Remembrance at the Anzac Memorial in Hyde Park commemorates those Australians and New Zealanders who died in World War I.*

Indonesia, and China. The economy of Australia benefited from increased trade with these countries.

Australia gradually dismantled its political and legal ties with Britain, too, emerging as a more independent and self-confident nation.

In the 1960s, Australia sent troops to the Vietnam War, and this brought big protests to the streets of Sydney. In the wake of this war and other conflicts in Southeast Asia came Asian immigrants — from Vietnam, Cambodia, Thailand, Hong Kong, and the Philippines — bringing new cultures and foods with them. Sydney changed quickly into the energetic, multicultural city it is today.

Back to Botany

Botany Bay, rejected for settlement in 1787, lies about 5 miles (8 km) due south of downtown Sydney. In the 1920s, it was developed as the site of an airfield, marking the new age of air travel. Today, it has a large container port as well, and commercial ships now dock there, deserting the downtown wharves of Sydney Harbour. The bay was originally named after its variety of plants, but the modern site is an environmental disaster area as a result of dredging, coastal erosion, and pollution.

CHAPTER 2

People of Sydney

The people of Sydney are known as "Sydneysiders." They come from many different ethnic backgrounds. However, the common language of the city and the nation is English, spoken with a drawled accent, the origins of which owe a lot to the Cockney speech of East London, England, where many of the early settlers came from.

The Aboriginal Population

Aborigines make up 1 percent of the Sydney population, the largest concentration of this scattered ethnic group in Australia. Their numbers are growing rapidly, boosted by an increasing number of people of mixed descent who are now proud to reclaim their Aboriginal ancestry. Sydney's Aborigines often describe themselves as "Koori," meaning "a person (or people) like us," and this term is now in general use. Kooris were denied the most basic civil rights until modern times and were not even allowed to vote until 1967. Since then, determined to regain rights to the land and win respect, some have made their name in sports, in the arts, or as social campaigners. Sadly, many Kooris are among the poorest Sydneysiders. Most live in the Redfern and La Perouse districts, often in run-down housing plagued by crime and alcoholism.

◄ *Aboriginal art is demonstrated by Clifford Possum at the Jinta Desert Art Gallery in Sydney.*

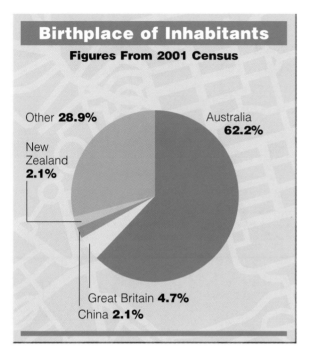

Birthplace of Inhabitants
Figures From 2001 Census

Other **28.9%**

Australia **62.2%**

New Zealand **2.1%**

Great Britain **4.7%**

China **2.1%**

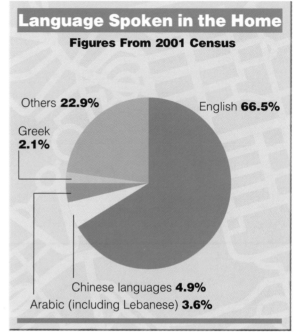

Language Spoken in the Home
Figures From 2001 Census

Others **22.9%**

English **66.5%**

Greek **2.1%**

Chinese languages **4.9%**

Arabic (including Lebanese) **3.6%**

▲ *In the ten years leading up to 2001, the proportion of Chinese-born people and Chinese-language speakers rose steadily. During the same period, the proportion of British-born residents and people speaking English as a first language fell slightly.*

"Strine"

Australian English has jokingly been called "Strine," a rough rendition of "Australian" as it is really pronounced. "Strine" includes many words from Aboriginal languages, as well as from English and Irish working men's slang of the 1800s and 1900s. Many words are shortened and then an "-o" or an "-ie" is added at the end, so "afternoon" becomes "arvo" and "costume" becomes "cozzie." This process also happens to Sydney place names, so "Paddington" becomes "Paddo."

Links with Britain

The history of Sydney has been dominated by continuous immigration from the British Isles. From 1947 until 1982, the Australian government offered cheap tickets to would-be immigrants. For £10 ($16) — about the price of a bicycle in the 1950s — emigrants could start a new life in Australia. Other Europeans and people from western Asia, such as the Lebanese, were invited to settle, too.

Even today, many Sydneysiders keep up strong family links with Britain. Because of this, the British make up a large proportion of the thousands of young backpackers who flock to Sydney each year.

Early Chinese Immigrants

The "gold rush" of the 1850s brought many Chinese people to Sydney, and today, more

17

Chinese people are arriving. Three Chinese-language newspapers are published in the city. The bustling Chinatown district is centered on Dixon Street, and the Chinese Garden near Darling Harbour is a gift to Sydneysiders from the southeastern Chinese city of Guangzhou.

New Immigrants

From 1901, immigration was officially restricted, the chief aim being to keep out nonwhites. In 1973, this racist "White Australia" policy was finally halted and Sydney became reenergized by newcomers, many of whom were highly skilled workers.

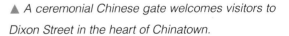

▲ A ceremonial Chinese gate welcomes visitors to Dixon Street in the heart of Chinatown.

Three out of every eight immigrants to Australia choose to live in Sydney. The city is now home to 180 ethnic minorities who speak 140 different languages. Major groups include Chinese, Italian, Lebanese, Greek, New Zealand, Indian, and Vietnamese people, but there are many other ethnic minorities. They include Maltese, Slavic, Kurdish, Afghani, Pakistani, Thai, Hong Kong Chinese, and Filipino people.

Many districts and suburbs have become established ethnic quarters. Leichhardt

"I think much of what the migrants did for us crept up on us, starting with things like food and wine and then gradually permeating through the entire culture — and immeasurably enriching it."

—Clive James, 2002.

▲ *Modern Sydney is ethnically diverse. These are Greek, Vietnamese, Maori (native New Zealand), and Aboriginal students at a public school in Redfern.*

is like a "Little Italy," while Surry Hills is full of Turkish and Lebanese restaurants. The most recent immigrants have settled farther out, with many Vietnamese and Cambodian people now living in the southwestern suburb of Cabramatta.

Racism is less marked in Sydney than in other parts of Australia, but recent disputes about asylum seekers and international politics have led to a rise in aggression toward Muslim communities in Sydney.

Christian Sydney

The traditional spirit beliefs and rituals of the Aborigines have been lost or disrupted in urban Sydney. However, they still underpin the social attitudes and views of the Koori population, many of whom are now nominally Christians. When one Koori woman was recently ordained as an Anglican priest, a smoke ceremony was used to dispel evil spirits, and she was painted with ocher as a symbol of purity.

From the first years of British settlement onward, Christianity spread across British-ruled Australia. On the edge of Hyde Park are the Protestant church of St. James (completed in 1824), and St. Mary's, an impressive Roman Catholic cathedral in the nineteenth-century Gothic style (begun in 1821). After a fire in 1865, St. Mary's was rebuilt. This is the headquarters of the Catholic Church in Australia. Sydney's Protestant cathedral, St. Andrew's (opened in 1868), stands on the corner of George Street and Bathurst Street, in the heart of the city.

Christian Festivals

Many Christian festivals have been brought to Sydney from Europe, such as the blessing of the fishing fleet in Darling Harbour each October, a Roman Catholic custom that originated in Italy. Christmas and Easter, the chief events in the Christian calendar, remain the most important public holidays. Australians celebrate the winter festival of Christmas (above) at the height of the southern summer.

English settlers brought with them the forms of Protestant worship known in Australia as Anglican, or in the United States as Episcopalian. Other forms of Protestantism were brought in by Scottish, Welsh, and Northern Irish people. Other Irish settlers brought the Roman Catholic faith, which was later reinforced by Italians and others.

For many years, there was a bitter divide between Protestants and Catholics. Since the 1960s, these old wounds have largely been healed. Many of the smaller churches have, since 1977, joined forces as the "Uniting Church." Some Greek and Slavic Christians follow their own Eastern Orthodox forms of worship, with many Greek Christians attending St. Nicholas' Church in Marrickville.

Sydney is home to about sixty thousand Jews, many of whom worship in the Great Synagogue on Elizabeth Street, built in 1878. Thousands of the city's Muslims gather to pray each Friday at the Lebanese Lakemba Centre or the Turkish Auburn Mosque. Buddhism, Hinduism, Taoism, and other Asian religions are growing in the city.

Ethnic Festivals

Many of Sydney's ethnic communities have their own street festivals and special days. In January or February each year, Sydney's Chinatown explodes with firecrackers and dragon and lion dances for the Chinese New Year festival. In late March, there are dragon-boat races across Darling Harbour, another Chinese tradition. Most city districts and suburbs have a day set aside for their own festival, carnival, or street fair. Irish Australians, and indeed anyone else who can enjoy drinking beer that has been dyed green, celebrate St. Patrick's Day on March 17 each year.

Food and Drink

Traditional Australian cuisine was once based on the worst of British cooking. Fifty years ago, a typical meal was made up of overcooked meat and vegetables and heavy puddings or cakes.

However, times have changed in Sydney, and now there is a taste for lighter, healthier food and a greater interest in flavors, spices, and salads. The chief reason for this has been the arrival of immigrants with their own methods of preparing and serving food — in their native Italian, Greek, Central European, Jewish, Turkish, Lebanese, Indian, Thai, Indonesian, Malay, Chinese, and Japanese styles.

Now a new type of Australian cooking draws on these many traditions and brings them together. There is no shortage of first-rate Australian produce, such as tropical fruits from Queensland and temperate fruits from Tasmania. There is shrimp; crab; lobster; all sorts of locally caught fish, such as shark; and freshwater crayfish (known as "yabbies"). Vegetarian food is popular in Sydney, but for most Australians, meat such as lamb or beef still makes up an important part of their diet. A few restaurants serve meat that would have been eaten in pre-European Australia — kangaroo, emu, or crocodile.

If tea was the favorite beverage in the age of the British Empire, the Italians have now brought good coffee to Sydney. Caffe latte, espresso with milk, is a favorite. Fresh vegetable and fruit juices, and "smoothies," are sold at juice bars and cafés.

Barbies and Beer

Thanks to the sunny weather, Sydney is the ideal spot for a "barbie" (barbecue). Steaks, kebabs, sausages, and seafood are all grilled in the open air in suburban gardens, at picnic sites, on beaches, or at outside bars, where customers can sometimes buy steaks to grill for themselves.

Vineyards have been a part of New South Wales for a century and a half. At many cheaper restaurants, diners can bring their own wine bottles. Australian "bottle-shops" (liquor stores) stock an even wider variety of home-produced wines than is seen abroad. They also sell vast amounts of beer, most of it light beers produced by breweries such as Toohey's or Foster's.

Most of Sydney's bars are called "hotels." Many are cavernous and noisy, with gambling machines, pool tables, and televised sports. They may provide food or snacks and entertainment in the form of loud pop music, jazz bands, or stand-up comedy.

CHAPTER 3

Living in Sydney

Australian folklore is rich in stories about the "outback," the arid interior of the land. Today, however, 85 percent of Australians live in towns and cities — and about 20 percent of those live in Sydney.

The Inner Suburbs

In inner suburbs from Paddington to Glebe are houses dating back to the nineteenth century. Some are large and spacious, while others are small town houses. Larger houses from around 1900 are set among shady eucalyptus trees where white cockatoos swoop and squawk. In the more expensive suburbs, there are modern apartments and courtyards draped with flowering bougainvillea vines.

In most suburbs, the architecture is less attractive with urban development dating from the 1890s to the 1930s lining the roads and railroad tracks. In these suburbs, you may see shabby rented accommodations, neat bungalows with small gardens, bars, and corner stores. In some areas, such as Redfern, there are run-down and vandalized apartment buildings littered with garbage and graffiti, and shelters for the homeless.

◀ *Small town houses with wrought-iron verandas, balconies, and railings still survive in inner suburbs such as Paddington. These intricate wrought-iron patterns are known as "Sydney lace."*

▲ The green lawns and shady trees of the Royal Botanic Gardens give office workers a relaxing break from the Central Business District.

The Outer Suburbs

The largest area of the outer suburbs, stretching westward, is occupied by street after street of red-roofed bungalows. The roads are broad with grassy shoulders, and houses have their own yards where children play ball and families host barbecues on weekends. Here, too, there are stores that specialize in products favored by the ethnic communities of their neighborhoods. On

Green Spaces

Sydney has large areas of parkland. The long belt of green that runs from the Royal Botanic Gardens through the Domain to Hyde Park is a precious resource, not just for office workers during their lunch hour but also for wildlife such as opossums (small, tree-climbing marsupials) and fruit bats. Centennial Park, below Paddington and Woollahra, is another great green spread, and there are smaller coastal parks such as Nielsen Park in Vaucluse. All provide a peaceful haven from the bustle of the city.

the land side of the city, the heat of the southern summer is more intense, unrelieved by sea breezes.

Shopping in Sydney

The most famous place to shop in Sydney is probably the Queen Victoria Building, on George Street. This lavish example of Victorian architecture was originally the city's chief fruit and vegetable market. Today, it is an arched shopping mall. Another splendid place to shop off George Street is the Strand Arcade, which dates from 1892. The Central Business District is where the city's main department stores are located. Designer-labeled clothing can be found on Castlereagh Street.

More typical of modern Sydney, but less fashionable, are stores offering crafts. On weekends, crafts, jewelry, clothes, and snacks also go on sale at many alternative markets. In Paddington Bazaar, a maze of stalls are crammed into a churchyard each Saturday, with fortune-tellers and street performers mixing with the bargain and craft hunters.

Food shopping in local stores or supermarkets follows the same pattern as in most cities of the developed world. Ethnic minorities have their own specialty stores, including Chinese supermarkets, Thai grocery stores, Italian delicatessens, and Greek bakeries.

◄ *The Queen Victoria Building houses about two hundred stores selling antiques, jewelry, and clothes.*

In the Fish Market

The Sydney Fish Market, off Pyrmont Bridge Road, claims to be the biggest fish market in the southern hemisphere and second only to Japanese markets on the Pacific Rim. The harbor fishing fleet off-loads one thousand crates a day to both trade and private purchasers. Auctions begin at 5:30 A.M. About one hundred different species of seafood are displayed on ice, and most are caught in local waters.

Transportation

Sydney's ferry boats, in green and white, leave the throng of Circular Quay carrying city commuters and tourists. There are also water taxis buzzing across the harbor and modern high-speed catamarans.

Circular Quay is also a bus terminus. Buses are the most popular way to get around inner Sydney, and regular users can buy a multiple-journey ticket that is stamped each time they get on the bus.

Traffic drives on the left side of the street, in the British style, and tends to be fast and aggressive. Traffic jams are common, and parking spaces are hard to find.

The city center is served by the useful City Circle railroad loop, which links Circular Quay with Central Station to the south and with the main suburban network. The trains are silver double-deckers.

▶ *A ferry leaves the Circular Quay landing dock, heading out below Sydney Harbour Bridge.*

The Monorail

An overhead monorail (above), dating from 1988, hurtles high above the streets between the downtown area and Darling Harbour. The track is about 2.5 miles (4 km) long and so it only makes a small contribution to the city's transportation needs. However, passengers can enjoy marvelous views of Darling Harbour and the sights of the Central Business District.

A new light railway line links Central Station on Eddy Avenue to the Pyrmont and Glebe districts.

Central Station is the terminus for inter-city express trains leaving for Brisbane, Canberra, and Melbourne. The Indian-Pacific service takes twenty-four hours to reach Adelaide and sixty-six hours to reach Perth, on the other side of Australia.

Shuttle buses leave from the downtown area and Central Station for Sydney's Kingsford Smith Airport (KSA), located in Mascot, a southern suburb beside Botany Bay. International destinations include flights to the United States and Europe, but many vacation flights are scheduled to nearer South Pacific and Southeast Asian destinations. Because of Australia's huge size, internal flights are the most common

"Slip, Slop, Slap"

Beaches and an open-air lifestyle are the big attractions of Sydney life, but pale northern European skin has not adapted to prolonged exposure to the sun. Ultraviolet rays can cause skin cancer, forming patches called melanomas. It was in Sydney that the connection of these patches with the intensity of sunlight was first established, in the 1950s. In New South Wales, one in 24 males and one in 36 females may expect to suffer from the disease by the age of 75. Today's youngsters are urged to cover up and wear a high-factor suntan lotion: SLIP on a shirt, SLOP on some sunscreen, and SLAP on a hat is the official advice. Elementary schoolchildren often wear hats with a flap to cover their necks.

▶ *A poster predicts a horror-film scenario for those who fail to protect themselves from the sun.*

method of cross-country travel. Located in Sydney's suburbs, the KSA site creates severe noise problems. In 1963, after many protests by residents, nighttime arrivals and departures began to be officially restricted. Today, no flights can take off after 11 P.M.

Health and Fitness

Sydney today has a good health record, with a life expectancy of 78 years for males and 83 for females (compared with 74 and 80 for the United States). Just over 5 in every 1,000 children die in their first year of life (compared with 6.5 in the United States). Infant mortality rates are in steady decline. Many Sydneysiders love outdoor activities and keep fit through exercise and sports. However, beer drinking is a way of life, too, and this can damage their health. As in many modern cities, there is air pollution from traffic and airplanes. Most heavy industries and other factories have now moved out of the downtown area, and, as a result, the air quality has improved.

Sydney has good hospitals and doctors. Under a national health plan called Medicare, hospital treatments are free. Visits to a physician must be paid for with a standard fee, part of which may then be paid back. There are also private health plans.

Sydney Society

Some say Australian social attitudes have their origins in the hardship and violence experienced by the convicts transported here in the 1800s and by the tough miners and sheep shearers and their long-suffering womenfolk. Their values have created a society of practical, down-to-earth, up-front people with a wry sense of humor.

However, times have changed since then, especially in cosmopolitan cities such as Sydney. Contrasting with the conventions of traditional Australian society, Sydney has a large and vocal gay community. The city also has a strong feminist movement dating back to the 1890s. Women gained the vote in Australia as early as 1902 and have played an important part in the political life of Sydney ever since.

Most Sydney families are small, as in the United States, although those people descended from Catholic or southern European cultures and traditions may have larger families, or extended families in which grandparents, aunts, and uncles keep in close contact. There is often tension between older and younger generations in immigrant communities where teenagers adopt the more materialistic lifestyle of their new country, which is famous for its surfing and partying.

Schools and Colleges

Sydney's education system is run by the state of New South Wales. Free schooling is offered for a minimum of nine years from ages 6 to 15. Most public schools are coeducational, and many schools require students to wear school uniforms. Students may leave after earning a junior certificate or stay to earn a senior certificate at age 17 or 18. Some study for senior certificates at separate senior schools.

Private schools are common and are often single sex. Many are faith-based, most often Roman Catholic or Anglican. Criticism of the growing inequality between private schools and state-run schools is growing. In state-run schools, there may be more than thirty students per class. Many parents would like that number to be brought down to the lower twenties.

A Grand Tour

Before or after attending college or applying for a job, many young Sydneysiders set off to see the world. Often, they journey overland through Asia to Europe, backpacking and traveling cheaply. When they arrive on the other side of the world, many look up distant relatives or get jobs in order to fund their return trip.

▲ *As school is over for the day, these uniformed pupils wait for the buses that will take them home.*

The school year is divided into four semesters with a short vacation between each semester. Emphasis is placed on applied science and design and on sports. Some school subjects reflect Australia's geographical location and its history. Chinese, Japanese, and Indonesian language lessons may be offered, as well as European foreign languages and Aboriginal studies.

Further Education

At age 17 or 18, pupils are ready to move on to a university or training college. The University of Sydney, with over forty thousand students, is the oldest in Australia and dates back to 1850. Centered south of Parramatta Road, the University of Sydney has many campuses around the city, such as the Sydney College of Fine Arts in Rozelle, the University of New South Wales in the eastern suburbs, Macquarie University in North Ryde, and the University of Technology in the Ultimo district.

Sydney at Work

Sydney's wealth was founded on farming, natural resources, and industry, as well as its harbor. The city is built on top of a coalfield, and a coal seam crossing below the harbor was formerly mined from the Balmain area. Today, the industrial heartland of New South Wales lies around Newcastle, a coal and steel city to the north of Sydney at the mouth of the Hunter River. Sydney, however, remains the big port, with container ships and tankers docking in Botany Bay. Exports include coal; metal ores; timber; and farming products, such as meat, wool, wheat, and fruit.

Industries and Services

Sydney's workforce makes up just over half of its population. Many Sydneysiders work in oil refineries or in factories producing electronics, metalwork, chemicals, paper, textiles, or garments. Food processing and brewing are also major industries.

However, nearly three-fourths of the Australian labor force now works in service industries such as banking, insurance, communication media, education, health-care, tourism, and administration. Nowhere has this switch been more apparent than in Sydney. The main occupations of workers

◀ *Officers stand together during a public protest in Sydney. Policing the city is the responsibility of the New South Wales Police Department.*

in Sydney's Central Business District and in the high-rise office buildings clustered around the northern end of the Harbour Bridge are banking, finance, insurance, and advertising. At the center of all commercial activity is the busy stock exchange on Bond Street.

A Changing Market

The city's overseas marketplace was formerly the British empire but is now the Pacific Rim. Today, business ties are likely to be as much with East Asian cities such as Djakarta, Kuala Lumpur, Singapore, Hong Kong, Seoul, and Tokyo, and with the west coast of the United States as with the European Union.

Main Occupations of Workers
Taken From 2001 Census

Others **37.8%**

Real Estate and Business Services **14.4%**

Retail Trade **13.4%**

Manufacturing **12.2%**

Health and Community Services **8.9%**

Construction **6.9%**

Education **6.4%**

▼ Railroad cars trundle past within sight of the Harbour Bridge. Sydney is still an industrial city.

▲ Since 1991, the number of people employed in real estate and business services has increased by 5 percent, more than in any other type of occupation.

The Koori Workforce

The unemployment rate has remained at between 5 and 7 percent, lower than for the rest of New South Wales and one of the lowest figures in all Australia. Kooris experience a much higher unemployment rate than the rest of the population, although they are more likely to find work in Sydney than elsewhere in New South Wales.

Messages and Media

The location of Sydney, far from foreign cities and on the edge of a large, sparsely populated land, has meant that in the past it has had to rely on mail and telephone services to avoid isolation. The hub of

Tourist Boom

Most visitors to Australia arrive in Sydney. The city receives about 4 million visitors a year, making tourism a major industry. Many tourists come from Asia. Japanese brides fly in to have their photograph taken against the beautiful backdrop of Sydney Harbour and the Opera House. While the big hotels cluster around the downtown area, suburbs abound in cheap hostels for young backpackers, many of them from Britain or Scandinavia.

▼ *Even in the age of e-mails, sorting the mail is a major task in a city of 4 million people.*

Media Moguls

Two men have dominated Sydney communication media in the last fifty years. Kerry Packer was born in Sydney in 1937. Packer inherited Australian Consolidated Press from his father, Frank. Kerry was the man behind Channel Nine broadcasting and at one time the Sydney Morning Herald. *Sydney is also the headquarters of Rupert Murdoch's giant News Corporation. Murdoch, too, was born into a newspaper owner's family, in Melbourne in 1931. He built a vast multimedia empire across Australia, the United States, Great Britain, and East Asia.*

Sydney's communications was once the General Post Office (GPO) headquarters on Martin Place. Today, in an age of electronic communications, this impressive building has been stripped and downgraded. The Internet has offered Sydney instant access to the rest of the nation and to the world.

Sydney is an important national and international media center. Big multimedia corporations play an important part not just in the city's economy, but in other aspects of life such as sports and entertainment. Many Sydneysiders eat breakfast while reading a copy of the *Sydney Morning Herald* or the *Daily Telegraph*, both Sydney-based daily newspapers with a national following, or the *The Australian*, a national daily newspaper.

The state-owned Australian Broadcasting Corporation (ABC) offers a wide range of news, music, and public service radio programs as well as Channel 2 television. Programs for ethnic minorities in many languages are provided by the Special Broadcasting Service. Commercial channels offer news, sports, game shows, and suburban-life soap operas.

City Government

Sydneysiders can vote at age eighteen — and they have to vote by law. The chief political parties in New South Wales are the Australian Labor Party, the Liberal Party, the National Party, the Australian Democrats, and the Greens.

Three levels of elected government apply to the city of Sydney. They often clash with each other. The top level is the government of the Commonwealth of Australia, which legislates for the whole nation. The national parliament is located in Canberra, 150 miles (240 km) to the south of Sydney.

The second level is the state government of New South Wales, which meets in the Parliament House on Sydney's Macquarie Street. It has wide powers within the state but cannot pass laws about national issues such as foreign policy. It includes an upper house (the Legislative Council) and a lower house (the Legislative Assembly). The forty-two members of the Legislative Council are elected from the state as a whole, while the ninety-six members of the Legislative Assembly represent constituencies (areas). Debates are often argumentative and loud. The public is often unimpressed, accusing their "pollies" (politicians) of being lazy or even corrupt.

The third level consists of local government, which is established by the authority of the State Parliament. There are forty-four city or municipal councils in the administrative divisions of Inner Sydney, Outer Sydney, and the Sydney Surrounds. Some people say that there are too many of them and complain of local bureaucracy. Local councils are elected every four years and pass local laws on city planning, traffic, hiking trails, garbage disposal, drainage, and other matters.

Sydney's oldest local council is the Sydney City Council. Its headquarters is Sydney Town Hall on George Street.

▼ *The Town Hall on George Street is a grand Victorian building with a clock tower that has been a downtown landmark since the 1870s.*

▲ *Traffic thunders from downtown toward the airport. Congestion and fumes present a growing problem to city planners.*

The City Council once had major powers, such as running the police department, but these are now mostly controlled by the State Parliament. The Sydney City Council has a publicly elected Lord Mayor, who represents the city at important functions.

The City's Problems

Sydney is a thriving city, but it does have serious problems. Environmental issues, such as longstanding arguments about the location of a new airport, are always evident. There is a considerable gap between the wealthy and the poor. In the City Council area, about thirty thousand homeless people need shelter. Run-down areas such as Redfern need renovations and new housing.

People Power

Since the 1960s, the appearance of Sydney has been transformed by new developments, such as buildings, tunnels, and streets. Many of these have been imaginative and successful; others have been disastrous, such as new roads and railroad tracks that have divided the city and cut through attractive districts. Increasingly, such projects have been fought over by builders, developers, and planning authorities on one side, and, on the other, by local residents' groups, environmentalists, and trade unions. One such dispute arose in Woolloomooloo in the 1970s. Campaigners saved the run-down but historic waterfront district from being taken over by high-rise buildings.

CHAPTER 5

Sydney at Play

Sydney contains a wide range of museums and galleries. Every other year, the city hosts an international exhibition of visual arts — the Biennale. The Art Gallery of New South Wales has a fine collection of European and Asian art, as well as Australian masterpieces, such as works by Sidney Nolan (1917–1992). Nolan was fascinated by Australian legends and folklore. The gallery's collection of Aboriginal paintings, inspired by ancient myths, is impressive. The Museum of Contemporary Art at Circular Quay West shows the works of many famous modern painters.

Performing Arts

If city dwellers want to see the Australian Ballet or Sydney Dance Company, they visit the Opera House. It has a concert hall, two theaters, and a stage for opera. The Sydney Symphony Orchestra often performs at the Town Hall. Many Australian musicians train at the Conservatorium of Music, located beside the Royal Botanic Gardens. Many classical concerts are held outdoors in the city's parks. The Manly district stages an international jazz festival in October.

Some of the city's best drama productions come from the Sydney Theatre

◀ *Tourists disembarking from cruise liners at Circular Quay can take pictures of historic replica ships or book trips around the harbor on pleasure boats.*

▲ *The Sydney City Council sponsors all sorts of lunchtime concerts in Martin Place for office workers, shoppers, and tourists to enjoy.*

Company, but there are a host of other groups, both traditional and experimental. The best-known downtown theaters are the Theatre Royal, the Capitol, and the State. The latter holds a movie festival each June, showcasing both international and

Australian directors. Australian movies have become popular around the world in recent years, and Sydney is a favorite location for moviemakers and movie festivals.

Authors and Books

One of Australia's best-known writers, Patrick White (1912–1990), lived near Sydney and wrote the Australian classics *The Tree of Man* (1954) and *Voss* (1957). Thomas Keneally, born in Sydney in 1935, told a tragic tale of Aboriginal life in *The Chant of Jimmy Blacksmith* (1972). His prizewinning novel *Schindler's Ark* (1982), about the fate of Jews in World War II, was made into the movie *Schindler's List* in 1994.

The State Library of New South Wales on Macquarie Street holds a writers' festival each May. July sees the Australian Book Fair, held in the Darling Harbour district.

Museums and Zoos

A day out for Sydneysiders could mean a visit to an exciting science museum called the Powerhouse; to the National Maritime Museum, which traces the history of sea travel from the Aboriginal era onward; or to the Australian Museum to find out about the weird and wonderful creatures that roamed this land in prehistoric times. For those who prefer to watch live animals, the Sydney Aquarium offers a glimpse of the colorful fish living around Australia's Great Barrier Reef. On the northern side of the harbor is the Taronga Zoo, which takes in wombats, koalas, and kangaroos — and crowds of Sydney children.

Fun and Festivals

Sydney's festivals and celebrations take many different forms. New Year's Eve is celebrated with fireworks over Sydney Harbour each year. In 2000, the blazing spectacle that heralded the new millennium impressed the whole world.

▼ At the Sydney Aquarium, visitors get a rare chance to safely view many of the marine species that lurk in Australia's deep-sea waters.

Australia Day

Australia's National Holiday is held on January 26. It is a public holiday marked by fireworks and concerts, including a big open-air pop music gathering. The date commemorates the arrival of the first British fleet in 1788. It is not generally celebrated by the city's Koori community, which holds its own festival of Aboriginal music.

Sydney's Mardi Gras, a gay festival held each February, has become one of the city's major international events, achieving widespread popularity. It lasts three weeks and includes art events, parties, and a spectacular costumed parade.

One of Sydney's oldest traditions is the Royal Easter Show, first held in Parramatta in 1823. It includes livestock judging, produce competitions, sheepdog trials, woodchopping contests, and carnival attractions. September brings the southern spring, marked by a kite-flying festival on Bondi Beach and by a celebration of flowers, music, and dance in the Royal Botanic Gardens.

Sporting Sydney

Like most Australians, Sydneysiders love sports. The city has produced some of the world's best sports stars, including swimmer Ian Thorpe. Anyone can join in the 9-mile (15-km) City to Surf road race from downtown to Bondi Beach. The annual race attracts thousands of amateur and professional runners each August.

Cricket is the city's oldest sport, having been played in Hyde Park as early as 1803. Today's Sydney Cricket Ground (SCG) is in Paddington. Cricket is played with bats and a hard leather ball on a grass field, with two teams of eleven players. The game is played from October to March and includes one-day matches, interstate matches in the Sheffield Shield competition, and international games called "test matches."

Australian football is played in a variety of forms. The most popular football game in Sydney is the rugby league, played district by district across the city. Interstate and international games are played in the Sydney Football Stadium in Moore Park. Rugby union is also played in the city. Both forms of rugby are played with an oval ball and the rules are very similar. A rugby league team has thirteen players, while a rugby union team has fifteen. Tough "Aussie Rules" football has also taken root in Sydney, with the Sydney Swans playing at the SCG. This game is a cross between rugby and soccer and is played on an oval field by two teams of eighteen players per side.

Australia has a National Basketball League, and the game attracts crowds to the Superdome in Homebush to watch the local teams — the Sydney Kings (men) and the Sydney Flames (women). There are many golf courses and tennis clubs all over the city. Horse racing is a big spectator sport, and Sydneysiders enjoy betting. The Melbourne Cup, run in Sydney in November, is the most popular horse race.

Olympics for All

Sydney was host to the Olympic Games in the year 2000. The contests were held in Homebush, west of downtown Sydney. Other Olympic locations included the Darling Harbour and Sydney Harbour. Some 10,300 international athletes came to Sydney. Aboriginal traditions were celebrated in the opening ceremony. There were also eleven Aborigines on Australia's national team, including the great Cathy Freeman, winner of the 400-meter track race.

Water Sports

As Sydney is an oceanside city, water sports are hugely popular. Many Sydneysiders can afford to go yachting, boating, and waterskiing. However, serious ocean racing requires big money. The most famous race is the Sydney-to-Hobart, which leaves each December 26 for the often stormy trip down to the south of Tasmania.

▼ *Stadium Australia is the centerpiece of the Olympic Park in Homebush. Home of the 2000 Olympic Games, it can seat 110,000 spectators.*

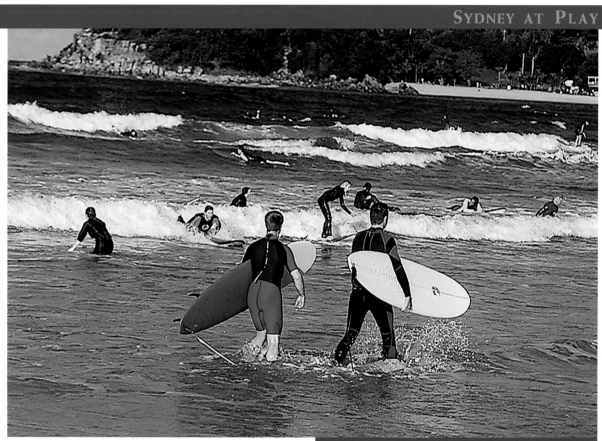

Surf Festivals

Surf festivals (above) take place on Sydney's beaches during the southern summer. These demonstrate lifesaving and swimming skills and the maneuvering of boats through the crashing surf. The muscle-bound lifeguards may be showing off, but their skills save many lives each year. The ocean waves, tides, and currents on Sydney's beaches are powerful and dangerous.

"Going to the beach is what summers are about. Sweltering behind closed doors and drawn blinds you can hang out for the southerly that won't come until midnight, sunbake in the backyard, stickier and stickier, try working, crankier and crankier or go to the beach. Hit the surf…"

—Meg Stewart, "Beachstruck on Bondi," from the anthology *Bondi*, 1984.

In addition to the harbor, there are about forty beaches and coves within an easy drive of downtown. Many offer clear water, sandy shores, and surf and are sometimes netted against shark attacks. Swimming and surfing have long been an essential part of everyday life in Sydney, and the rolling breakers of the Tasman Sea cannot be topped for surfing. The Bondi Surf Bathers' Life Saving Club was founded at Bondi Beach in 1906, and this has become one of the most famous surfing spots in the world.

CHAPTER 6

Looking Forward

"Sydney has the air of a place whose moment has come."

—Bill Bryson, American travel writer, 2000.

By the middle of this century, the population of Sydney is expected to rise to about 6.5 million and then level off. Sydney, for so long the city of sprawling suburbs and bungalows, is literally moving up. A soaring eighty-three-story apartment building, the World Tower, is being constructed on the corner of George Street and Liverpool Street. High-rise construction is expected to spread far beyond the Central Business District to the outer suburbs.

Transportation Problems

Skyscrapers are of no use if the streets below are gridlocked, however, and that is the fear of planners. Transportation management will have to be a city priority, and the site of a new city airport must be part of that plan. Whether the solution is a second airport in western Sydney or a site far out of the city with a fast railway link remains a matter of debate. Some argue that larger planes with more efficient fuel systems will mean that a single site could remain viable.

◀ *Sydney is not a paradise for all its citizens. Many homeless people must sell magazines on the streets to earn money.*

The Asian Link

The economic future of Sydney will depend on the fortunes of the Asian and Pacific Rim nations. At the same time, an increasingly high percentage of the city's population will be of Asian descent. As links with Asia grow, Australia's ties with Great Britain become weaker. The desire for Australia to become a republic is strong in Sydney, and it seems likely that the British flag will soon disappear from the state flag of New South Wales.

Aboriginal Rights

About thirty years ago, another flag began to be flown in Australia. Colored red, black, and yellow, the flag was adopted by the Aboriginal people as part of their campaign for land rights. The city of Sydney will not truly be at ease with itself until it has come

▲ *Aboriginal actors stage a play for schoolchildren in order to educate a new generation about ancient Aboriginal beliefs.*

to terms with the people whose ancestors paddled their canoes along the Parramatta mangroves and the coves of Port Jackson, spearing fish and painting rock.

A Promising Future

Sydney has come a long way since James Cook first spied the dunes of Botany Bay through his telescope in 1770. The city has grown considerably and, in the last thirty years, has transformed from a backwater of the world's far south into a modern, high-energy city. Sydney is now expected to become Australia's economic capital — the powerhouse driving the entire country.

Time Line

c. 50,000 B.C. Aborigines settle in what will become New South Wales, Australia.

A.D. 1770 English navigator James Cook anchors in Botany Bay and claims the land for Great Britain.

1788 The first fleet of British convicts arrives in January. Captain Arthur Phillip locates the penal colony in Sydney Cove.

1793 The first free settlers arrive in Sydney.

1810–21 Lachlan Macquarie's governorship of New South Wales brings law and order.

1816 The Royal Botanic Gardens are laid out by Macquarie.

1832–51 The British government sponsors migration to New South Wales.

1840 The last convicts arrive in Sydney.

1850 The University of Sydney is founded.

1851 A gold rush in New South Wales brings Chinese people to Sydney.

1901 New South Wales becomes a state of the new Commonwealth of Australia.

1914–18 Sydney's men fight for the British Empire in World War I.

1920s An airfield developed near Botany Bay marks the new age of air travel.

1925 Sydney's population passes the 1 million mark.

1929–34 Sydney suffers great hardship in the depression years.

1932 The Sydney Harbour Bridge is completed.

1942 Japanese submarines attack ships moored in Sydney during World War II.

1947 The end of World War II triggers a new wave of immigration from Europe.

1963 Sydney's population passes the 2 million mark.

1973 The controversial Sydney Opera House is completed.

1973 The end of the "White Australia" immigration policy is followed by immigration to Sydney by Asian refugees.

1988 A monorail between downtown and the Darling Harbour is completed.

2000 Sydney stages the Olympic Games.

Glossary

arcade a group of shops that are connected by a covered walkway or avenue.

asylum seekers people who arrive in a country not their own and ask to stay because they would be persecuted in their own countries.

bureaucracy in government, too much administration and management with too little accountability.

coastal erosion the wearing down or washing away of a coastline by waves, currents or winds.

colony a settlement of people from one country in another land, or a land or region governed by another country.

corruption dishonesty in government or business.

cosmopolitan coming from many parts of the world.

dredging removing sand or mud from a seabed or riverbed.

Eastern Orthodox describes a Christian tradition of worship originating in Greece, Russia, and Western Asia.

environment surroundings, especially the natural world.

ethnic background, shared descent, or culture, as exemplified in language, customs, or religion.

European Union the largest and most powerful economic and political union of nations in Europe.

flying boat an aircraft whose main body forms a hull, so that it can take off or land on water.

immunity resistance to a disease.

materialistic nonspiritual, concerned with matter or money.

mogul a powerful leader within a particular industry (originally, a Muslim emperor of India).

Pacific Rim the regions and coasts bordering the Pacific Ocean, especially when viewed in an economic or political context.

paddle steamer a steamship propelled by large paddle wheels on the sides or the stern.

pollution the poisoning of land, water, or air by human activity such as industry, transportation, or agriculture.

profiteering making excessive profits by taking advantage of the public need, as in times of war, hunger, or shortages.

Protestant describes a Christian tradition of worship deriving from those who broke away from the Catholic Church in Europe in the 1500s.

quay a wharf or pier used for docking, loading, or unloading ships.

radical literally, going to the root of a problem: therefore, favoring drastic political action or reform.

republic a government ruled by a president or head of state, not a monarch; citizens elect their own public officials.

Roman Catholic describes a Christian tradition of worship headed by the Pope in Rome.

terminus the end station of a railroad line, especially a large city station.

textiles cloth produced by machine- or hand-weaving.

trade union a federation of workers within a workplace or an industry who campaign for improved wages or working conditions.

Further Information

Books

Banting, Erinn. *Australia the Culture (Lands, Peoples, and Cultures)*. Crabtree Publishing, 2002.

Bartlett, Anne. *Aboriginal Peoples of Australia (First Peoples)*. Lerner Publishing, 2001.

Godwin, Beth. *Livewire Investigates: The Sydney Harbour Bridge*. Cambridge University Press, 2003.

Pember, Brett. *Livewire Investigates: The Sydney Opera House*. Cambridge University Press, 2003.

Sharp, Anne Wallace. *Australia (Indigenous Peoples of the World)*. Lucent Books, 2002.

Stein, R. Conrad. *Sydney (Cities of the World)*. Children's Press, 1998.

Web Sites

www.cityofsydney.nsw.gov.au
Official web site for Sydney, with details of events, businesses, development, environment, and history.

www.sydneyoperahouse.com/h/kids
The official web site of the Sydney Opera House.

www.phm.gov.au/observe
The Sydney Observatory site with information about the southern sky and astronomy in general.

www.nationalparks.nsw.gov.au/npws.nsf/Content/Home
The New South Wales National Parks and Wildlife Service site with natural and Aboriginal history, Australian animal and plant information, and more.

www.phm.gov.au/exhibits
Sydney's Powerhouse Museum site with innovative science and design exhibits online.

www.austmus.gov.au/features/index.cfm
The Australian Museum online with loads of information about Australia's geography, natural science, and biology.

Index